automatic lighthouse

the second
tall-lighthouse
poetry review

tall-lighthouse

tall-lighthouse wishes to sincerely thank all of the poets for contributing their poems to this review. We also offer our gratitude to all the poets who have read for us at our events and those that have submitted their work to us.

tall-lighthouse logo designed by mat andrew

ISBN 1 904551 24 6
published 2006, reprinted 2007
www.tall-lighthouse.co.uk

This is the second tall-lighthouse poetry review, a continuing celebration of contemporary poetry.

It contains a wide selection of poetry and poetic styles, performance and page poets in equal measure. It features a number of poets who have read for us at our regular events in London, Brighton and Exeter, poets whose work we admire, new translations, as well as poetry from America, Holland and Italy.

We are pleased to include poetry from some old friends from the first review, Jamie McKendrick, Maurice Riordan, Sarah Maguire, Andy Brown together with a number of tall-lighthouse poets. We also welcome new poems from Hugo Williams, Lee Harwood, Brendan Cleary, Catherine Smith, Michael Laskey and Roddy Lumsden together with work from a number of fine young poets including Fiona Benson, Jacob Sam-La Rose and Helen Mort.

We trust this anthology will stimulate interest and debate for the new voices featured as well as confirming the stature of the more established poets.

tall-lighthouse

On Thursday 26th November 1998 the last manned lighthouse in the UK was *switched off*, the North Foreland lighthouse in Kent, subsequently all UK lighthouses are now *automatic lighthouses.*

contents

Catherine Smith	The Full English	1
	Celery	2
John McCullough	Unbreaking a Stone	3
	Coombeland	4
Michael Laskey	The Page-turner	5
	Fried Potatoes	6
	Terminus	7
Carole Hawkins	Mrs Rogét	8
Anthony Wilson	Poem to Myself	9
	After Doisneau	10
Carrie Etter	After and Before	11
	When We	12
Hugo Williams	Tangles	13
	Black Samurai	14
	Last Things	15
Timothy J Wesley	Punched Drunk	16
David Trame	Myths	17
Maureen McManus	Christmas	18
Helen Mort	Photograph of My Mother at Twenty	19
	Chopsticks	20
	Litton Mill	21
Janice Fixter	Sillage	22
	A Kind of Slow Motion	23
	Blinding	24
David Crystal	A Brockley Night Bird	25
	The Bone Factory	26
	Bird of Ash	28
Jamie McKendrick	Five Poems by Valerio Magrelli	
	With cogs	29
	I've often imagined	29
	With the passage of time	30
	Often the page	30
	Interrupted sleep	31
Maggie Sullivan	Odds	32
	House rules	33
	Soundings	34
Philip Ruthen	Radio News	35
	Jean-Paul were you truthful	36
Maggie Sawkins	Chasers	37
Nell Grey	Guerrilla Warfare	38
	Humanity in the Guise of Insects	39
Maurice Riordan	Mediums	40
	[he begins with a line by CJ]	41
Fiona Benson	Harvest	42
	Convento Dos Capuchos	43
	Cuckoo	44

Anne Rouse	The Verbals	45
Lee Harwood	A small bundle	
	Ornithology	46
	Continents	47
	Parsley	48
	Objects on a Polish table	49
Kathy Wrightson	Back Kitchen	50
Andy Brown	Three poems from *Goose Music*	
	iv *My brother Audubon*	51
	v *Heron chick*	52
	vi *Scattering my brother's ashes*	54
Luke Heeley	Travelling to Delphi	55
	The Cup of Coffee	56
	Removals	57
Rachel Kann	this precise desire	58
	learning how and why	59
Marc Swan	Azure Night	60
	Through a window darkly	61
	Three Calls	62
Aoife Mannix	Broken Love Waltz	63
Isobel Dixon	Lamb	66
	Struggle	68
James Bell	*from* The Just Vanished Place	69
Jacob Sam-La Rose	The Edits	72
	Never	73
Santana	For You	74
	My Father's Brother	75
Kim Lasky	*from* What it means to fall	76
Cathy Ryan	Longing	78
	Ache	79
Jack Hayter	Horsey Girl	80
	Into the Tardis	81
Ronnie McGrath	Pink Ribbons	82
	Skin	83
Roger Robinson	Glenda's Big Decision	84
	Hog Plum Tree	86
Abdul Jamal	Inside the Wardrobe	88
Ros Barber	First Man Out	89
Heather Taylor	Halloween in Winter	90
	Immigrants	91
Frank Diamand	*from* The breaking of a heart - how it is done	92
Luke Kennard	Ear	94
	Eyes	95
	Mouth	96
Lisa Dart	Failing Light	97

Pierre Ringwald	Bear	98
Alex Brockhurst	By the pool	100
	Costa Brava	101
Graham Buchan	The Bank	102
Brendan Cleary	Out take	103
	Stepping Out	104
	Sunday Afternoon	105
Keith Please	Minaret	106
	Whale Watch	107
Sarah Maguire	To Damme and Back	108
Tom Chivers	White Buildings	110
	Letter to Barry McSweeney	112
Roddy Lumsden	Tyrol	113
Clare Pollard	Hell	114
James Byrne	The Lighthouse	116

the poets (brief biographies)   i - v

The Full English
Catherine Smith

It's been said that whoever gazes upon a plate
of bacon and eggs, has, in their heart,
already committed breakfast. In which case

I've committed the swallowing of succulent mango,
the gorging of fresh, fibrous pineapple,
I'm guilty of dribbling papaya juice down my chin

with shoals of muscular, dark-skinned boys
who flip from quivering diving boards into
early morning pools. And, furthermore,

I've committed the stirring of porridge, the slicing
of a slightly over-ripe Fair-Trade banana,
the drizzling of honey, with the quiet man

on the seven forty-seven from Brighton to Victoria,
who crosses his legs to match the way
I cross mine, who shakes out his *Guardian*

as though it's a clean bed-sheet. And when
I find you - and I'll know at once it's you,
by the low rumble in my belly - I'll go for

the Full English: fried eggs with frilled edges,
bacon, dark, oily mushrooms, sausages, tomatoes,
toast and tea - cup after cup of sweet, milky tea.

Celery
Catherine Smith

You used to hate it - so pale and skinny-ribbed,
like the sleeve of a sensible light-weight sweater.
It's virtuous, parsimonious, it contains so
few calories you burn more energy eating it
than you take in. Bossy muscled women
in Health and Fitness magazines order you
to crunch it raw, steam it, stir-fry it briskly.
When you do, it tastes of water - or of glum,
salt-less afternoons at a Welsh great-aunt's,
the crack of it exploding rudely in your mouth
like gunfire from a distant trench.
It tastes of all those diets you went on
in your late teens, when you agonised
about your arse and thighs, when you adored
the Minister's son, the engineering student,
the snake-hipped photographer who posed you
against railings on wet Sunday afternoons....
but today you read an article on boosting
sex-drive and find celery is wonderful,
that it stimulates the pituitary gland,
contains two pheromones that cause arousal!
Celery is a sex aid, and all you need to do is
lie back, relax, snap a stalk, shake off the
water droplets, ease open the top button
of your jeans, stroke your belly and crunch,
let the fibrous strands snag your teeth,
wait for the chemicals to work their magic,
then ring your lover on his mobile
- bad timing, forbidden, because he's currently
standing by while his wife blow-torches
individual Crème Brule's for their guests -
and, with your mouth full of fibrous aphrodisiac,
ask him, *Hey, guess what I'm doing?*

Unbreaking a Stone
John McCullough

With you asleep, I sneak downstairs
and pass the night in the company of geodes.
Each has a story, some hollow: a nothingness
I can read the world through. My favourites
violet and cream: boiled sweet bands
that wall in a crystalline core so furious
it's like looking down on a thunderstorm.

But there was no kind way of bringing it
to this room. It had to be smuggled
out of that river, coaxed open with a hammer.
And let's not pretend the earth doesn't fracture
itself every day, lay bare its heart to send minerals
bubbling up like kisses. Some centres must burst
to make their beauty known.

Like us, reunited after your flight, squeezing
each other's hands on holiday inside a honeycomb
of cool, crumbling limestone we penetrated
together: a Bronze Age labyrinth that smudged
bone tools malachite-green. Those miners
craved the pith of sealed ground too, hauled it up
in splinters to prize it in more generous light.

I steal back to bed, the moonlit embryo of you,
fitting myself against your warm curves
and thinking not of the morning's bright hammer
but a darkness deeper and colder than this,
a river never swum, blacker, more unearthly
than Lethe with winding spectres for fishes
and geodes, blissful geodes, dreaming underneath.

Coombeland
John McCullough

Work of the devil. Dark place where hills
mould men. Where sense and breath adjust
to a muscular camber, the ground's diaphragm,
small houses riding contractions, stiff verbs.

Chalk ridges give the dialects backbone.
The hole-ridden earth draws in watery vowels.
Ploughshares bring up guttural relics,
flint-teeth with the sibilant ocean inside.

Stroke a nugget of chalk. Already white dust
accents the contours of your fingertips. You inhabit
the past tense, submit to a crumbling tongue

the way the hard *c* in *coombe* yields
to liquid and the unsayable ghost of a *b*
that's the beat of the land's hollow heart.

The Page-turner
Michael Laskey

He sits in her shadow, keeps still
as if he would be as invisible
to us as we are to him,
just his eyes imperceptibly moving

till the end of the page approaches,
when, rising from his chair, he reaches
forward, left-handed, and works
a single sheet free, then waits

for the moment to flip it over.
Pressing it flat with his palm
from below so it won't lift up,
already he's pushed himself back

out of consideration. Again and again.
Till the pianist bows, and he stands
apart disclaiming applause,
head down, holding the music.

Fried Potatoes

Michael Laskey

Say the magic words and she's standing
interminably at the stove turning them
with a small kitchen knife
and that cooking fork Suki took,
its silver plating worn off
and its tines of uneven length bent
as if wanting to be her left hand
with the crooked little finger we couldn't
straighten, broken and badly set
years before she was our mother
by some fool of a doctor, a fall
at tennis did it or Zip her beloved
bull terrier tripped her? Stories
I wish I could check, but never
thought much of then, being young
and hopeful, too full of my own
hunger even to know I was watching
the dollop of dripping beginning
to slide in the hot pan, to melt,
to clarify what it meant
to be her, here, all but transparent
with Dad gone off and us going,
cutting the leftover cold
boiled potatoes into slices
that sizzle, spit a little as she turns
them over. How long till they're done?

Terminus
Michael Laskey

I may come back I'm afraid
as a faded floral curtain
hanging at the window of a flat
overlooking a city station
yard, the clangour and grind
of shunting, corrugated iron
fences and engine sheds.
The curtain will stay closed
always. Behind it in the room
lit by a single off-centre
ceiling light – a double bed,
twisted sheets, an implacable succession
of bodies, sagging bellies, armpits,
anuses, audible pain
the curtain will have to keep facing.

Mrs Rogét

Carole Hawkins

I use only one word
when one will do –
not him, he uses lots –
and I'm peeling the carrots,
my feet like ice –
I say *Get some coal on the fire dear*
but he's on a flow and I know
what to expect –
But darling, sweetheart, love ...
then I fume, but relent,
Get a grip, grasp, hold –
of the scuttle please,
and obtain, bring, fetch
the fuel, fire fodder ... coal?'

But –
on occasions
he chooses fewer syllables
to display his intentions –
just catches my eye
with his best transfix...
So I look towards the ceiling
as he breathes -
Lets slip out of syntax
into something more revealing -
so I gather his perception
and remove my blesséd apron.

Poem to Myself

Anthony Wilson

This stuff you've been giving us recently
about the fledgling flailing atop a duster
just will not do. Likewise your description
of its body: were its eyes mahogany,
I mean, actually? Also, why is its bib
a Victorian's beard? And the way you spring
it upwards, as if after a slip catch:
why must cricket keep appearing in your work?
I am anxious, too, as to your state of mind.
Questions such as Will I last?
or How do I compare with - ?
lead only to madness, jealousy and paranoia,
you must know that by now. By all means
read the beautiful poets, if you think it will help.
But you know as well as I do you often
lack sleep for days afterwards.
Go where your energy is:
those who say you found your voice
too early 'perhaps' are cretins
and need spanking.
As Jim says, you are much funnier
than you think and much better company
when you bounce! You know
you are going to die one day, what difference
will it make if you are the one in class
whose stones don't skim perfectly?

After Doisneau
Anthony Wilson

It is late afternoon in the capital,
mid-century perfect for lacing oneself
upright on a bench (noises-off: *boules*

clacking in the dust) and watching the line
of trees mist then disappear under
the *Tour* whose arches ring

to a crocodile of pedal-horses towed
by a head-bowed bereted man picturing
his mistress bored with waiting.

After and Before
Carrie Etter

Under scant light, in sharpening air,
a coyote noses the gulch's rabbit holes,
and a boy sprints from parking lot to
field to lot again, touching the black rack
from which my bike was stolen. The
coyote, raising his head, fixes his gaze.
Sensible of each breath, each blink, I.
The sun drops as a brusque breeze lifts
fine hairs, as someone practices violin in
one of the upper apartments. Words
slowly pool. The outdoor lights flicker
into a pale glow, vermilion stripes the
horizon, and the boy pants, resting his
hands on bent knees.   I could not have
apologised any sooner.

When We

Carrie Etter

My skin began to shimmer, and I realised that the light had arisen within and was showing at my pores. It was like receiving a letter from someone I'd never written to but always admired at a distance. It was like receiving the responses to every letter I'd ever subvocalised but not transcribed, thousands from my mother, a lapful from forgotten childhood friends, dishevelled stacks from one or two particularly gentle former lovers, and from you, a long, mahogany desk overspread with shifting hills. I reminded myself to exhale, blurry with certainty in the widening solace.

Tangles

Hugo Williams

I have been practising stroking your hair
the way you like it,
not running my fingers through it
and getting caught in all the tangles,
just rubbing lightly over your head
the way your mother used to do it,
without ever getting tired.

I have been sitting here for so long,
practising stroking your hair,
I have almost got the hang of it by now.
I do it the way you taught me,
not too hard and not too soft.
I think you would be proud
to see the progress I've made.

Black Samurai
Hugo Williams

Enter the Black Samurai,
wielding a Samurai sword,
uttering Samurai cries.
In a single circular exercise
he opens a window
in the front of your skull.
You glimpse, through crimson rain,
a loved expression,
a smile that closes up one eye.
As darkness descends,
it all comes back to you -
her face, her voice, her skin.
You taste on her tongue
the horror of lost joy.

Last Things

Hugo Williams

I stand on a little rise
watching the long grasses swaying.
Chaos rules over there
where the last things are.
I scan the horizon,
scenting them on the wind.

A drone starts up in my head
as of insects nesting.
In the lull before the storm
last things hang back.
They jostle one another
getting ready to be born.

When the wind changes direction
they have no choice but to happen.
Now one of them breaks cover,
makes a sudden dash.
Will it be my last swim?
Or my last Greta Garbo film?

Punched Drunk
Timothy J Wesley

Meeting of two heads
clash where no speech is given
the total time is seven
and of course the canvas is *red*.
With interest I listened
to the radio waves
as they gradually glisten
as one colour bursts out of another
crying his pain
in agreement they invisibly are
about this race
their race
and our race
and what they'd be doing
if they weren't
face to face.
Soon you will hear
if it is fair when it's over
one head is dumb-struck forever
and of course the colour is *red*.

Myths
David Trame

Enduring flashes. You sprayed the guests
one by one with the bottle of seltzer,
moving it clockwise around the table,
you took your time before each face
sensing the glow of your inward smile,
the sprayed water a marvel expanding
a deluge with just this small hand pushing
and the sudden grimaces on countenances,
cheeks dripping, mum's, aunt's, granny's,
eyes closed, tightly, skin with long furrows
stretched suddenly like a puzzle.
Someone smiled then, some showed
mild outrage, except your father,
you got a glance of burning rage
but fear was still far
on that continent, on the afternoon
of one of your first birthdays,
your cousins upturning
a small wooden table, glossy
brown and polished, lamps lit
a moon travelling, you sat
on that platform cross-legged
while they pushed you around in a frenzy,
the world slid smooth, the hall a field
of lightened marble. Sparks.
Bits of you. Bits of your front teeth
when you slipped and fell laughing,
mouth open, but no cries then, just
your face flushing with relief
when you realised you could still whistle.
The whistling tune of a golden age.
Fringes of a dream teetering,
the outward shore of a continent now
whose clamours haven't been
hushed yet
by the stirrings of dawn.

Christmas

Maureen McManus

Your voice on the phone was like holly,
spiky with red berries,
like Christmas white
feathery snow and cold brightness:
the sound of bells on a horse drawn sled,
a cinnamon stick of hard sweetness,
the crisp cold heights of a slope,
territory of the sublime
a white-out dry-out heaven
on the line.

Photograph of My Mother at Twenty

Helen Mort

She must have smelled of wet pine needles,
a thick pelt of them under her walking boots,
though the valley's near treeless.
September, perhaps, the end of the holidays,
and she's got her weekend face on; crinkles
and eyeshadow, flashing a hand-me-down smile.
In her left hand a raincoat, in her right,
where the cigarette should be,
someone else's fingers. Blue polyester,
slate-thick rain, the camera's swipe
catching him at the shoulder blade

like the sluice of windscreen wipers,
keeping this from that, the dim sweep
of these headlamps, the shapes beyond them
as I drive through suburbs, and, casual,
in the shadows a girl with red stilettos,
her walk a needle's stutter,
drawn through the night again and again,
the thread pulling taut between us.

Chopsticks

Helen Mort

We're not afraid of giants. It's gossamer
that unsettles us, cotton thread.
Not the brightness of this winter sun,
but the thin gauze of our eyelids.
I remember your sister's flat,
the moth in the kitchen window
no-one would release
for fear of snapping its wings.
You turned in your sleep that night,
a cocoon of warm skin, and
I didn't know how to touch you.
Remember the skaters, surfing sky

and tarmac, snatching at the delicate air,
for a second, hanging there.
We found a park, an artist making a mountain
out of chopstick pyramids.
We helped him build a haystack,
saw our throws take flight,
watched the whole thing avalanche
at the touch of a small boy.
And when at last it came to ground,
there was the sound of skateboard wheels,
a stirring like moth wings in the air
and no-one to say who's hand
it was that really brought it down.

Litton Mill

Helen Mort

Hold me, you said,
the way a glove is held by water.
Black, fingerless, we'd watched it
clutch a path across the pond,
never sure if it was water or wool
that clung fast.
The mills are plush apartments now,
flanked by stiff-backed chimneys
and you ache for living voices,
the clank and jostle of machinery,
for something to move in this glassy pool
where once, you were the waterwheel,
I, the dull silver it must
catch and release
as if it can't be held.

Sillage

*The scent that lingers in the air when a person
who is wearing perfume passes by*

Janice Fixter

Inhale the mist and I am there,
this other life,

following her trail through O levels,
parties, a Janis Ian soundtrack.

The musk of it all
barely contained.

She, who I once was,
the schoolgirl almost come of age.

Essence of her,
escaping from this gold topped phial,

brown as muscovado now.
Inhale again.

Eighteen, leaving school for the final time
she pauses at the gate,

as if someone is behind her,
as if someone just out of sight is watching her.

She shivers,
catches the scent of something new in the air.

A Kind of Slow Motion
Janice Fixter

Step out of the morning,
walk along the hunch of pebbles,

button your coat against the cold
and watch the single canoeist scull

between the dip and dive of gulls.
See the light change -

cloud shadow float on waves.
Slip into a kind of slow motion.

Choose a pebble,
smooth or glinting quartz,

lick its salt,
taste the union of ocean and stone

before you drop it in your pocket.
And it will surprise you

on a day when the air is stale
and almost too thick to breathe

and you are fumbling for keys,
a train ticket, a handkerchief.

But for now keep it secret
and leave the slow suck of sea

and the winter chill to find a café.
Order a cup of Guatemalan Cloud Forest.

Let the steam warm your fingers, your face -
feel the blood rush.

Blinding
Janice Fixter

We are chasing bats
with a million candle torch

burning up the sky,
blurring stars

that have long imploded,
sucking matter into black holes.

And the bats flit from pine trees,
small enough to be pipistrelle,

disrupted from the plunge of night,

calling to each other
in a spirit language rich and out of reach.

Caught in this blinding together
we strain our eyes
to become reflective as a fox's -

reconnecting to the metaphors of dark.

At 4am I turn the hall light off,
night seeps beneath the door of every room -

across your face while you sleep,
across my hands, my feet.

I locate the bed, my place in it,
listening to your breathing.

A Brockley Night Bird
David Crystal

After the cold spell, a week into the New Year
a bird warmed its throat singing through the night
from two till dawn. Sleep impossible,
impossible sleep the bird lived inside my head,
like a Miles solo till day break.
Walking for milk with murder in mind
I passed the Somalian Ali-Gab Café.
A Somalian elder called me over.
He gave me a little bottle.
This will cure the jazz bird.
How did you know? He ignored my disbelief,
and walked into the café, joining friends under
the waterfall mural. He was right.
I soaked bread with the potion
and left the bowl near our mint and wild garlic.
The bird must have feasted well
for I slept dreaming of blue feet,
my grandfathers blue feet, watching
him build a fire mouthing the words
of his favourite song *After the ball was over,*
Nellie took out her glass eye...
swirling around the smoking stack
that morning at the Crem, a swallow,
the bird on his chest he could never forget,
free at last.

The Bone Factory

A poem written after reading Edwin Muir's Autobiography.
David Crystal

Bosch. Breughal. This is Hell.
I'm the clerk in a suit of decaying meat
looking at the world through a wall of glass.
A moving snowdrift of laughing seagulls
picks my bones clean most nights.
The other clerks dream a paradise of girls
on islands with no rain or snow.

One hot June day the yardman
fought new Catholic hires working the furnace
their skulls split open with greasy bones
fat with yellow maggots. Old Doyle
looked at me with a wink stirring his viscous tea
with a tiny dried chicken bone.

Father from our cramped Crosshill tenement
you longed for Kirkwall, the heron's
                                    slow deliberate flight
seals calling for lost souls,
that special smell of Orkney wind.
I know Glasgow finished you.
No secret places to fish
you couldn't understand keys or that beggars
had to be turned away from your door.

Father as a child I often watched you
talking to yourself, happiest re-inventing stories
faricks dancing on the shoreline
ghosts from the sea making us scared of bed.

Father my soul is weary, my dream notebook
                                        full of doom.

One whisky night I stood by the canal,
                                  ready to jump
the death spell sunk by a man playing a fiddle
above a shoal of mouthing trout. I walked on,
kicking a stone onto the moons full silver face,
flakes of ash nesting on a lonely swan
your voice fading with the fiddlers broken song.

Bird of Ash

David Crystal
(9/11 in memory of Elizabeth Irving)

up in smoke
       she to went that day
  a six minute service
          the same Glen Miller tune as
Arthur

ashes
launched
     into the air
        the way you would launch a bird
into the wild beyond after sickness or injury

    at a Quayside bar
        we watched the drama on Sky News

all that is solid melts into air

  ash dust bones gold

     wing waltz memory with a swooping crow

six eggs-brown
        no brisket this week

riding up and down
        her second hand Stannah
Johnny from next door

  daft as a brush as she always used to say.

Five Poems by Valerio Magrelli
translated by Jamie McKendrick

With cogs

With cogs, tiny levers and teeth
the clock seems a chariot armed with scythes
to rip the day to bits – it rends
the day's corpse, tears its joints and tendons,
shreds the hours, bones them, as night's
rotation uproots
the sky's light and strips bare
numbers, figures, frameworks,
the shining cloudy skeleton
of the constellations.
So, x-rayed, the body
retires, at low tide,
uncovers its bed, the underlying
lowlands, the mountain tops,
the dormant fossils
beneath light's healthy flesh tones.

I've often imagined

I've often imagined that looks
outlive the act of seeing
as though they were poles
with measurable trajectories, lances
hurled in a battle.
Then I think that in a room just left
lines of this kind must stay
poised and criss-crossed for some time
maintaining,
cross-hatched, intact,
their complex integrity
like a needly haystack
or a game of pick-up-sticks.

With the passage of time

With the passage of time all the milk
goes bad, as though
it had turned evil.
It contracts, solidifies,
sloughs off its proper liquid form,
assumes a body, revived
in new compact flesh, extracted
from the beast. It turns to
cheese, a metamorphosis
into an occult creature, the dead
fruit off a living plant,
a pale sated lunar being.

Often the page

Often the page lies becalmed.
It's futile turning it to find
what quarter the wind
might blow from.
Nothing moves.
Thought wavers in that calm.
Things wrecked and
torn asunder there
by navigation
painfully repair themselves.

Interrupted sleep

Interrupted sleep whistles and creaks,
a snapped branch that bares
green virgin wood – it's broken clean
but the sundered parts remain
held together
by a long white fibre,
meek, shivering, undefended,
the plant's heart and soul,
its tendon.

Odds
Maggie Sullivan

We've lost the knack of keeping socks in pairs.
There's another stray under the bed
dusty and down at heel, its twin
abandoned in a drawer somewhere for lack
of a companion.

They go recklessly solo,
slouch off down the side of the settee,
refuse to stay together on the washing line,
one decomposes in a flower bed
and here's Homer Simpson tucked
at the back of the wardrobe
pining for Marge.

I gather them in,
lay them out on the bed like corpses,
the sober black and grey, already in mourning,
spots and stripes all at sevens, no sixes.
When did we stop counting in even numbers?

Today, only one pair remains, scrunched
at the bottom of the laundry basket
in a last desperate embrace.

House rules
Maggie Sullivan

You entered
and the house reacted like an insecure child.
That tap I thought I'd fixed
resumed its drip, drip, drip
of anxious interrogation.
Ghosts in the cellar whispered
'Is he safe? Can he be trusted?'
Knives unsheathed themselves from
                                      kitchen drawers,
turned blade side up.
My bed demanded identification.

This need to know, in advance
the exact duration of your visit,
all the intentions –
that old broom beating its tattoo
what is love, what is love, what is love
precisely?
Pots and pans in constant dispute
with the dishwasher.

We keep strict time here.
Clocks stopped - the key
lost the means to wind them on,
what the mirror reflects, faith shattered.
The calendar always assumes an end date.

Never say 'You'll find out'
that's death to the rug,
no gaps in my cupboards
though I like the way you open them,
handle an oil can,
approach the fridge unafraid

and you have won over the duvet.
It has warmed to the way you slip
your hand under my left breast
each night, bring it to rest
over my heart, as if to say 'You can break now'.

Soundings

Maggie Sullivan

The guide book insists Venice is sinking.
We are walking by a canal at night.
Beneath the surface I can see the city's future
perfectly reflected, its grandeur and
dilapidation;
the Ponti di Sespiri breathing
its last on the lagoon bed,
the bells we heard ring out
in the Campanile di San Marco
rusted and silent,
the shimmer of a gondola adrift
without oarsman or lovers.

For you I, still rising to each other,
Venice floats fragile, unfounded.
We turn the pages,
take soundings above
and below the water line.

Radio News
Philip Ruthen

The worst time in the day is 1.50AM
When there's no-one to draw my empty breath
To craft the call of longing from the beat

To sleep; frozen to the radio's claim
What else is left?
The worst time in the day is 1.50AM

Duty drives my words' scattered aim
On a page not yet kept
To craft the call of longing from the beat

Across the wires, florid pain
Out-lined, now kept,
The worst time in the day is 1.50AM

You must be elsewhere, that daylight's claim
Safe gathered, but left
To craft the call of longing from the beat

I decide after elsewhere what will remain
When there's no-one to draw my empty breath
The worst time in the day is 1.50AM
To craft the call of longing from the beat.

Jean-Paul were you truthful
Philip Ruthen

I found a card
that had never been opened
in the wicker picnic basket
the card reads
'being is what it is'
and Sartre is named
beneath a brush-stroked icon
as a leaf alights
on the accompanied stone
for an instant
and although this image
brings pleasure
what could be free floating
is the breeze held on rocks
and later labelled.

Chasers *(for Brendan Cleary)*
Maggie Sawkins

The morning after the concert party
and I catch him pouring whisky into his tea.
He's talking poetry and women –
the ones he's lost to horses and drink.
And because he reminds me
I tell him about my ex –
how when things got bad
he'd come back from the bookies
so flustered you'd think he'd been chasing
a horse by the name of 'Love's Tail'
around the track. He pours another
Talisker's, I sip my gin – think about
the years it takes to get out –
the split breath to fall in.

Guerrilla Warfare
Nell Grey

If I run without fear
in the darkness,
a dew appears on my face,
neck and arms.
Then the moon comes, stars pierce
the upturned hull of sky
and I remember
the machine-gun rattle
of the woodpecker
the morning you left,
your sleeping body riddled
with dreams,
the way you stuttered her name
like confession under the screw.

Where are you now?
At rest perhaps, rocked
in your wooden ark,
calmed by the soft whinny of a mare,
the rough tongue of a bitch,
clawed awake by a she-cat.

There's nowhere
to hide. This same moon
that sees me now can see you too;
these hard stars can make a stone
of a woman unless
she runs in the darkness

and never looks back.

Humanity in the Guise of Insects
Nell Grey

A wasp slices the softening air;
the hottest hour has passed
and ripe plums send a golden string
to draw her into yellow
drunkenness.

She will fill that dark place,
her tongue quivering
as she drinks away
the taste of duty;
of a fly's wings cut,
discarded,
the body chewed,
spat out
to nourish larvae.

What drives her?
Is it the drops of sweetness
given in exchange?

Or can it be that underneath
her sharp striped suit,
her ruthless competence,
some hidden part trembles
at her role as hunter –
ordained not chosen –
finding in the amber nectar
some small release
from the high glass sky.

Mediums Acts 2: 13
Maurice Riordan

He drank only *mejums* on his outings
to marts, funerals, race meetings.
After a few he'd break into song.
A few more and he spoke in tongues.

[he begins with a line by CJ]
Maurice Riordan

I didn't get where I am by wearing underpants
        decorated with Beethoven.
Or the Red Flag, my father said. Or even the
        Turin Shroud.
I didn't get where I am on the Orient Express.
I didn't get where I am by taking
        night-classes in Chinese.
I didn't get where I am by taking my eye
        off the ball,
by putting the cart in front of the horse
        or by turning the other cheek.
I didn't get where I am eating figs
        and olives and gherkins.
I didn't get where I am in Malibu.
I didn't get where I am with yoga, feng shui,
        cranial massage, or acupuncture.
I didn't get where I am in wigwams.
I didn't get where I am on the snows of Kilimanjaro,
        or on a pilgrimage to Saint James of
        Compestela.
Nor did I get where I am because your mother
        prayed every night to St Jude.
I didn't get where I am beholden to any man.
I didn't get where I am at the Fleadh Ceoil.
I didn't get where I am at the Munster Final.
I didn't get where I am at the Sorbonne.
I didn't get where I am in pub, club or club-house.
I didn't get where I am on the camel's back.
Nor did I get where I am in the Order of the
        Golden Dawn,
or by joining the Royal Society for
        the Protection of Bullshit.
I didn't get where I am by thinking it would all
        sound a lot better
in Italian, that you could put a tune to it
if only it were in Aramaic or Mandarin Chinese.
No, that's not how I got where I am.

41

Harvest

Fiona Benson

All August rain, then summer's heat;
now this unbearable weight –
pears dissolve on the branch,
the orchard's glut of apples and plums
rots in the grass.

Out here where we walk
it's hips and haws,
brambles that loosen in the sun,
blacken into full bloom,
become juice on the stalk.

I taste all this on your tongue
as, dragged down to the wet ground,
we waste ourselves again,
lost to the summons of this old need,
this flaring into thistledown; pod, bract, seed.

Convento Dos Capuchos
Fiona Benson

All the long road up
sunlight throbs between pine
and the heat is resinous, dry.

Then this clearing,
thin air shining
in the reclaimed garden,

sandy floor, slow pond,
idle carp a dull gold,
Feverfew, St Johns Wort...

Hollowed into the rock
a honeycomb monastery
lined with cork,

the walls still warm in the dark.
I could sleep in the stop
between leaf and sap,

winter it out
sleeved in the sound
of the wind in the firs

and the dangerous passage of angels.

Cuckoo

Fiona Benson

Fresh-hatched, damp, this gowk
shuffled up your clutch egg by egg,
weighed each one in the dip beneath her neck,
then shrugged them over the edge.

You didn't suspect, even when
her flesh strained your perch,
her cleft gape triggering
your endless fetch.

She ground you up, made bread.
You won't see spring,
while she will beat her way south
beginning it again,

priming nests with her young
to leave rogue and fugitive;
her own blood shunned,
sapped by the haemorrhage.

The Verbals
Anne Rouse

Rejecting even the word, *mistake*,
(the glass cobweb on the new specs,
lost French book, scabbed knee)
by thirty I'd digested another word, *foibles.*

Then at mid-life, the word, failings, appeared
in the other's mouth. Cranky guard of a glass house,
bluff, or rudeness – once you'd have thought, all-this
but oh my failings, what would I be without you?

Stuck in a fault; pinioned to a sky of stone.

A small bundle
Lee Harwood

Ornithology

A wall of dense fog ahead
- blocked, all knowledge denied.
'The flying bird brings the message'
What message from out there?
(Chirpy chirpy cheep cheep doesn't help much)

Flying low it sweeps over the meadows

hunting small insects then moves on
heading north to settle
for a while.

The worn book advises small steps
and a slow care. Nothing too fancy.
Some form of change ahead, it says.

A silence on the hillside. All this whiteness.
A stillness in which time has ceased, or seems so.

As the mist shifts you see swallows set on a wire,
a wagtail bobbing on a rock.

Continents

To praise
your hand resting on the table
your forehead   timeless

To be so 'transported' by love
so that each detail of a day
becomes a marvel

To long for this is no-crime

*

At midnight the full moon hazy
a single star to its right
with a soft sweet breeze
brushing the balcony
a sweep of sea off in the darkness

*

A silk dressing gown slides from your body
as you stand in a moonlit garden
the scent of roses
many hours away   many miles away

*

We line up to walk the plank
but

Parsley

The old man travelled home on the bus
holding a small bunch of herbs,
every so often putting the parsley to his nose
to smell its scents.

To describe this is more to do with wonder
than the sentimental.

Objects on a Polish table

1

Four books, two newspapers,
an ashtray, a pack of cigarettes, matches

2

when visitors are coming
some poppy seed cake or doughnuts
or fresh baked makaroniki
placed on a plate on the table

a lace table cloth beneath the coffee cups

3

a ceramic salt bowl with a lid

4

an empty vase in the centre of
the oil cloth

come and sit down

Back Kitchen
Kathy Wrightson

A heavy farmhouse table with carved,
castored legs, chenille cloth covering
the cup marks and the cranking handle
for the extension; oddments of chairs,
roundwood and spindle-backed, some
squashed with cushions, a black-leaded range
with red-tiled side oven, now baking towels;
flanking cupboards, baby-sitting armies of
Farrahs Harrogate toffee tins, bulging
with buttons and old foreign coins:
"*Your grandfather brought them back
in his merchant navy days*";
Victorian curling tongs bent on burning,
gas oven hot for singeing her hair,
under-cupboard drawers,
sticking and straining –
hiding the light from blue, pink
and white hyacinth bulbs
laid down for the winter.

Three poems from *Goose Music*
Andy Brown

IV   My brother Audubon

The bird he sees and the bird he draws
are one. Which begs an inner silence,
shifting from the world of words
to the language of tone and line.

He must forget the names he knows –
neither 'tail' nor 'wing', nor 'beak' nor 'claw' –
and simply move along the edge of each,
with his eye set in his pencil-tip,

thinking of no sound at all – save that of ink
on paper – to catch the truth
of their existence, out there, in the world.

A buzzard flaps overhead,
clutching something dead.
He catches it in chiaroscuro.

V   Heron chick

We stepped into morning
through snaggles of moss
        and toadstools,

our memories of the times
        we'd been before

laid out beneath us
        like flagstones in a path.

Evidence of otters –
a pair we knew
were somewhere round –

in the form of fish heads,
abandoned on the verge.

You pushed through
thickets of Indian Balsam
clogging the bank,
their swollen seedpods
                going off
like strings of firecrackers –

a kingfisher clattered by in blue,
hunting dace and minnow –

and I stood back,
looking through
        the swathe you'd cut
            in them.

There was the heron chick,
bedded down between the rotting logs –

broken, it's wing
        and it's legs…

'Nature is a common link' they say,
so why would *You* or *I* lift up a hand

to put the chick out of its misery,
while the other argued we should simply leave

with no interference at all? In spite
of all the things we both might choose to say,

both ways were the same;
                          and *there* lay our bond.

VI   Scattering my brother's ashes

The sea pulled us through an interior
of tractors turning perfect furrows open
to seagulls flocking in their hundreds, worming;

down to a bay where we walked untouched
sand, alone, save for the tracks of waders
and distant children dipping nets for schools
of fingerlings in the shadows of rocks.

Hopeful boats hung on the mud bars, waiting
for the tide to rise and take them out
into the crescent of the sky-mirroring sea.

The sun lay low – falling in erratic islands
of light. You tipped and emptied the urn
with a fierce grief – a moment of oneness –
knowing that by evening the estuary would turn.

Travelling To Delphi
Luke Heeley

Our driver knew the secret of the mountains,
the moment to swing us away from the sheer fall
to a river melting through rocks and pines.

After holding the hours in our lungs, we reached
the monastery: deserted, it seemed,
                                        except for a cat
sunning its belly in the herb border. The city,

with its cola rain and parade of headless
                                        demi-gods,
unravelled behind us. We threaded
from the shade of one hotel lobby to the next.

In a darkened room, we witnessed
                                        the transformation
of Ouzo into smoke and sipped the potion, later
hiding the bottle beneath an upturned dinghy:

by morning it had gone. Poseidon had necked
                                        the dregs,
split on a joyride round the islands.
We wound on, mazing towards the morning

when our destination arrived as a dream.
In its thin air, we raced against the athletes:
dipped, breathless, over an invisible line.

The Cup of Coffee
Luke Heeley

Sipped with care or knocked back like hemlock
it begins its silent transaction within you.

From beneath those foamy reefs, an undercurrent
blooms into the outline of a car

as it draws towards a no-horse town
that sees no business but survives through winter;

while in the alpine hideaway a lamp comes on,
revealing the laughing teeth of your nemesis.

Already the henchman is shaking on his overcoat
and turning up the collar. Even now

the dark grail is travelling towards your lips
through the impossible mountain pass.

Removals

Luke Heeley

Now the cherry tree has kept its promise,
gathering from the jackhammered earth
                              that glow
which lights its leaves from within,
we're ready to quit this scene.
Books untanned by oxygen
are boxed and taped. Stripped
of our small print, these rooms
which we know so well that they're forgotten
have grown as large as first thoughts.
Our departure takes place inch by inch
as we deliver ourselves to the boot and the van.

The woman who lived downstairs
died there two years ago; and when they came
to clear the flat, they left
her furniture, dresses, letters by this drive
to flap and blur in the rain
then turn to mulch.
                              Returning late
I met the silhouetted glance of a fox
before it slinked into the wildness of roses
that had been her garden; soon though,
the council men came for its body, swept away
what remained of its almost human cry.

this precise desire
Rachel Kann

each night i discover him anew
buried in blue fluid
face up and supine and i trawl him
towards the shore

on the packed sand,
wipe away the wet
careful-palmed

thumb open his lids
gentler than breath
wait, patient, for eyes to flicker
into recognition

fingerpart familiar lips

watch in wonder while
he remembers breathing

ache with adoration for
his rise-and-fall chest

this hunger is unprecedented

this precise desire

i stretch my weariness
against him

let the water lap our
ankles like hungry flowers

> when the moon tumbles
> and morning cracks
> me open, i am ever alone again,
> evaporated, holding nothing
> dreaming of sea anemones
> and belonging.

learning how and why

Rachel Kann

now, i cannot tell you his name or breed, but
i can tell you he was huge and tan and curly-
furred, his owner was an old man in a navy
greek fisherman's cap, that i puppy-loved
him, how his dog-strong back felt under my
miniature hand, and autumn early-evenings
my father and i ventured the three-quarter
block to pacheco elementary school where
i would roll around the blacktop resplendent
in my standard-issue white-with-red-and-
blue-stripes-roller skates, de rigueur for any
five year old girl in nineteen seventy-eight,
and sometimes curly-tan would be there too,
he was dog enough for me to hold on his
leash and let him drag me, gliding over
hopscotch and four-square demarcations
like i couldn't be fenced in. like i was
somebody special.

now, i cannot tell you what it felt like inside a
father-heart to watch such a thing, but i can
tell you he made his arms a cradle for my
skate-heavy clanking-ankled body and
spirited me home, laid me on my bed and
unlaced them while my face bled, that my
mother cleaned that burning, within
moments i had availed myself of a rare
escape-hatch afforded to children and fled
the scene by falling asleep, curly-tan had
been pulling me, it was blissful until wheel
kissed rock, i faceplanted into asphalt, he
had his back to me, kept right on running,
i covered ground like that until synapses at
long last snapped to attention and brain sent
word to my hand, that holding on was not
helping. how it echoes, strained begs over
blacktop, my father's voice:

let go

Azure Night
Marc Swan

She flies down the gutter on her belly,
head high, bright red sleeve frayed
and snarling at the wind.
This is not a game, but a chance
encounter with a remarkable ending.
She is barely injured, a tear
in the flesh of her forearm, cracked
bone. It will mend easily
as the red sleeve. I carry
her unaware of eighty-five pounds
in my two arms to a rickety slip
where a man in a Redskins cap
jauntily tilted back off his wide
forehead greets us, directs me
to a cabin where she will rest
while he steers this ancient Chris
Craft over the tumbling water
of Puget Sound. I know his voice,
the tone, the way he says *he she*.
I think of his last book of poems,
sharing pages with Chekhov,
of his last ten years - *Pure Gravy*,
he said. *And don't forget it*.
From this momentary earthly
interlude, he will soon return
to the infinite writing retreat
in the sky with Fante, Bukowski,
Breece D'J Pancake -- to name a few.

Through a window darkly

Marc Swan

He takes out his nail clipper
slides open the blade
plunges the file
deep into his calf
We have been talking of golf
and the war
the lack of feeling below
his left knee
how he is on the links
of Buffalo
year round
"cold doesn't bother me"
"I don't golf," I say
"hip injury"
After the blood stops
spurting thanks
to his ever-blonde wife
he tells me to leave
"I don't like you," he says
"I don't want you around my daughter"
I am nineteen
life a puzzle with a gap
where, for some, hubris is alive
I drove one hundred and twenty miles
that day to pick her up
I drive one hundred and twenty miles
home   My mother listens
to my 2 am rant
never saying a word
I read something in her Irish eyes
You will write of this later
and of other things you cannot change.

Three Calls

Marc Swan

There was blood in my semen he says
when I ask of his recent medical visit.
He tells me they went in with a probe
and sliced seven pieces of flesh out of
that quiet organ with the walnut shape
hidden deep in the soft folds of his rectum.
The next call is a job offer, quite unexpected,
punctuated with the fact that I have one week
to make a decision. The third is of another
kind, this time my wife answers. A neighbor
has called about another neighbor, a quiet,
attractive single mom with big eyes full of
wonderment who discovered her fifteen-year
old son hanging in her garage. I have no words
to say when my wife tells me this between gasps
and sighs and eyes wide with the confusion
that accompanies a parent's worse nightmare.
I told my friend with the bloody semen
that my heart was with him, that there are
treatments now that far exceed our imaginings.
I imagine they won't be necessary I tell him.
It is the karma thing I operate under. The job,
it is the right offer for the wrong company,
and I will deal with that another time, but the
child, the barely adolescent I spoke to last
week after the blizzard as he tromped through
three feet of snow making his way home – what
words are there in the lexicon of human kindness
that can make any difference at all.

Broken Love Waltz
Aoife Mannix

You were my hero, my reason for life.
What did I care for history, all those silent
graves. I tried to get you to listen to our
happiness, but your heart was always
somewhere else. I gave you a paradise of
white horses and eternal sunshine, but you
spat it back in my face. I guess I never
understood the greenness of your pride,
the hollow ache of all that homesickness. It
seemed to eat you from the inside, like a
cancer, like a language I couldn't speak.
I tried to warn you the centuries were
passing, but you insisted on going back.
Of course the moment your feet touched
the ground, the reality of it hit you. Without
love, you were just another tired old man.

Are you with me today my love
Are you with me today my love
I'm waiting for you to come back home
And never leave me again.

Don't be silly Willy, I never wanted to tread
on your dreams. I had my own lover at
home, and he smelt of gun powder and
lightly burnt toast. He didn't talk much, his
smiles were all choked with revolution. He
spent his nights sleeping in ditches, his
uniform a poor excuse for foolishness.
I wish I'd had your way with words but the
sad truth is that all the beautiful poetry in
the world won't turn a heart around when
it's bent on suicide. The red wine of blood,
all those stupid songs, capturing the
castle. I searched for him in the ruins,
turning over the corpses of young boys.
I stared at their empty faces, and it made
me so angry.

So don't talk to me of romantic Ireland when kids have no shoes and the only thing keeping their mother alive is the pint of Guinness after giving birth to their thirteenth child. When I heard they'd executed him, I felt as if my soul had died, and now I'm a martyr's widow, don't speak to me of pride.

Are you with me today my love
Are you with me today my love
I'm waiting for you to come back home
And never leave me again.

He told me he wasn't a criminal, that's why he wouldn't put on the prison uniform. I said what does it matter what you wear, since when were you so concerned with fashion? That at least made him smile, though it vanished when I informed him the only thing he was a victim of was his own stupidity. I regret those words now, the way they seemed to sink into his wasted flesh. I shouldn't have pointed out he was half the man he used to be, but it was true. His bones cutting through his skin, his face like a mask of the man I loved. But his eyes, his eyes seemed to burn right through me. He said the priest had been in to see him but he'd told him to go to hell, he wasn't ready for last rites. Then eat something I begged, why should you be the one that's sacrificed? He said I didn't understand and he was right. How does starving yourself correct an injustice? Hundreds of years they kept us hungry, now they want to force feed me. He laughed softly, he always had the most beautiful laugh, and he never lost his sense of irony.

They buried him with a full gun salute from the men in balaclavas, all of whom looked perfectly well fed. It's not so much that I'm bitter, more broken hearted, and sometimes in this country it's hard to tell the difference.

Are you with me today my love
Are you with me today my love
I'm waiting for you to come back home
                    And never leave me again.

Lamb
Isobel Dixon

We left him sleeping peaceful in the night
but they have tied him down, bony wrists
wrapped in a sheepskin cuff,
                              lashed tightly to the rail.

He was fierce after we left, they say:
shouting, tearing at the drip. Hard to believe it
of this gentle man, but this morning,

unbound for the time we're there, he cavils,
clawing at the needle in his arm, moaning
and stubborn, baring his teeth at us

when we refuse. I stroke his fettered hand,
his paper forehead, murmur comfort,
courage, anything. He shakes me off, tossing

his head, red-eyed, an angry ram. Ha!
I must remember who I am: his child,
just a child, why do I question him?

So I hold my tongue, but stay. Lift up the cup,
with its candy-striped concertina straw,
to his splintered lip and he, in resignation, sucks.

Yes, we make a meagre congregation, father,
disobedient. The flesh, indeed, is weak.
Still, remembered echoes of his sermons come:

a promised child, the tangled ram,
                              the sheep-clothed son;
last-minute rescues, legacies, and lies.
The promised and the chosen, certain hopes.

How, from these stories, are we to be wise?
His word was clear and sure before, but now
his raging, rambling, shakes this listener's heart.

And yet, to be here, of some small use,
is a kind of peace. Three spoons of food,
oil for his hands, his feet. Then at last,
at last, returning to gentleness, he sleeps.

Struggle

Isobel Dixon

The matron's jaw is clenched,
her mouth sealed tight. Reluctantly,
she tears a narrow smile from it.
A line slit with a paperknife.

We're locked in battle.
This is her proud vessel,
she's the captain of this ship
and now my father's under her command.
We're nothing to her
but a band of stowaways,
ornery women, rocking the boat.
I half expect she'll send us packing,
off to scrub the deck,
these endless, polished passageways.
But no, I'm staying by his side, on watch.

He lies between us, sleeping,
covered by a sheet.
Across this ravaged territory
I meet her prim, efficient gaze.
I note a flicker – yes, she knows
there's more of us – my sisters,
bold as pirates, tireless, brave.
At last, I see the titan give.

Stay, then, she says.

James Bell

what can we celebrate
if there is nothing to begin
with - *is* is not positive

an implosion with grave
consequences neither can
cure with a simple smile

silent cinema with distances
of time - stark black and white
in the greyness of winter

*

this could be only words
without much substance where
no feeling to become reality

exists in riddles and codes
only you understand - have
not touched a universal note

will not join up to make
music - symphonic or
minimalist - engaged in silence

*

it is good to be stung
by a bitter wind that
lashes with words
you understand yet
cannot comprehend apart
from the element of
blame looking for a
target with bent bullets
you call stingers

*

so what is so good
to be stood upon by

the interests held by others

anothers who stand tense
with steel and words

stolen for what is called rational

to feed their own madness
inside an imagined circus

where there are still animals

*

less unified we stick
together - hands heads
and bodies as nowfill
physical or metaphysical
even as words spoken
or crammed on a page
entire in a momentary
embrace called entwine
found in all endfill

*

what you call a dead duck -
really must be if it lies
in the mud at the waters edge
while a crow makes generous pecks
at some exposed flesh
and could well call it dinner

nature is impressive with its
displays of naked dispassion -

you look at this death a long time

*

*

and did that make
grammatical sense and is
this in first second or
third person and does
it follow any discernable
rules that can be placed
on pomes - this is the
question and this is the
answer - no - not really

*

The Edits
Jacob Sam-La Rose

She wants him in a smaller package.
Exactly him – same voice,
same penchant for graphic novels
and toast that's just turned golden

brown, same way his hand smoothes
her back; but with edits. Prettier
eyes. A more flattering chin.

A taste for Kate Bush, or at least
a modest talent for interesting dinners
and household chores, a knack
for fixing pipes.

In this world, she's settling
for what she has – the voice,
the hand – and she's happy.

In some alternate world,
she's alone. In another,
they've married and divorced
– the children call another man *dad*.

In yet another, he doesn't exist.
She's found the eyes she always wanted,
and everything else falls into place.

Some nights, she wakes on the shore
of his sleep, lulled by the tide
of his breath, echoes of other realities
ringing in her ears.

Never

Jacob Sam-La Rose

He never taught me how to hold
a pair of clippers. I never saw him
dab cologne on his cheeks. I don't know
the smell of his sweat, or if our fingers
look alike. I didn't learn to drink
by draining whatever wine he might have left
or sharing an ice cold can. He never
wrestled me down, so I never grew up
to return the favour. I didn't learn to love
music thumbing through his vinyl LPs.
I never woke him. He never once raised
his voice at me. I never heard him laugh,
and although I remember him at the end
of a long distance call, once,
I don't remember his voice,
or what it might have sounded like
saying my name.

For You
Santana

Boogie called me up Sunday night,
said his auntie needed the car back,
told me how life ain't been fruit snacks
since rent and broken transmissions.
Said he don't know
how he gonna get to work tomorrow.

I tell him I'm shaking just like he is…
fingernails jagged from time clocks
and cash register keys,
I tell him this is Chicago.
We gotta work just to see the stars.
Squint eyes to part fog like cornrows.
I know it's tough, Boog,
but squint harder
and you'll notice the moon cart wheels
off horizons and tomorrow comes.

Just wait till January; I'll get the car back
and take you to a little patch of grass
up by the lakefront and there,
there we'll dance to gunshots
and Lake Michigan
under planets that spin
for you, me,
and anyone with a 9-5,
anyone who has ever been stopped by cops
for being alive,
and for the girl spittin' poems on stage
just to get by,
squint hard…
and you'll see, for us,
the moon dances itself asleep,
and brings tomorrow.

My Father's Brother

Santana

I.
They dared his aim.
Bet a pack of cigarettes
he couldn't crack
the old jibaro's window
three houses down.

He pulled back
a tan leather pouch
tied to bacon-thick rubber bands.

Marbles: ammo.
Let go.

> My father's brother,
> Junior, killed a man
> with a slingshot.

II.
Now, he paces across Viequez.
Gathers coconuts
from orphaned trees,
sells them for a dollar.

Only left his business to visit
his mother's funeral back in St.Thomas
where he gave me a t-shirt he made -
"Se Venden Cocos."

I tell him he'd make more money
if he sold the shirts.

> He says nothing,
> teeth rotten
> from letting go.

from **What it means to fall**
Kim Lasky

I

Outside intrudes:
the walled garden, the horse chestnut,
the way green leaves turn yellow
from the outside in, lie brittle-thin,

tinder-dry, ready to tear at the touch
of a single stone on a gravel path;
the claw of a passing bird.

Inside her head there are sand dunes,
a red kite trying to catch the wind.

II

On the Downs trees are losing leaves,
impressionist curves shifting to straight lines,
the angular shape of a Picasso landscape.

Shadows are darkening into squares,
green into grey into black, linear,
stacked, like stairs ascending
or descending.

This is the planned accident of a brush stroke;
a single leaf dropping silently at night,
unseen by the semi-circular slice
of a waning gouache moon.

III

Like an astronaut cocooned on the quiet side
of the moon, watching the way a rock hammer
and a falcon's feather drop together minus
gravity,
she gathers facts.

IV

$$v_a = \frac{1}{2}gt$$

is the mathematical equation for a falling body,
the key to her average velocity

under constant acceleration
for any given time; in theory.

In reality things get in the way:
the earth's invisible spin, resistance,

things that impede constancy;
like memory, the smell of vanilla ice-cream

melting over fingers.

Longing
Cathy Ryan

What if she slipped into my bed late at night
hovered over me, her hand barely touching
my back as she moved over my outline,
gently sensing my heat, wanting to lightly
touch the skin of my whole body
moving her foot against my foot
and kissing my body with her
tongue.

What if she rolled me over
and looked at my face
my breasts
my belly
my sex
happy
erotic
still…

Ache

Cathy Ryan

i

Your mouth when we kiss
pulls me in, along, through.

What are we looking for?

ii

Your passion stretches your neck back
                              over the bed
your body hungry to arch to the ground
as you rise to my hand

iii

Waking up this morning beside you
you weren't there

Where have we gone?

Horsey Girl
Jack Hayter

I guess
you'd be the darkest one

maybe more like the shadow
of a stallion

or a river

you would be the still one
perhaps running so deep
I would need to rent a bathyscaphe

Into the Tardis
Jack Hayter

All of the billions of lovers
over these hundreds of thousands of years

inarticulate

gasping for air

saying the dumbest thing
at the tenderest moment

like   I never knew your hair
would be so soft   shhhh

or

hey you're so warm   stairs
            maybe just   up
                        lets go

Pink Ribbons
Ronnie McGrath

The cracked silence
seeps out of an egg shell & into my heart

I can rest now, lying in this bed of mine
wrapped around my lady

the two of us knotted like the
red festivities of pink ribbons

arm against leg, tits against bum
nostrils pushed into each others hair

an elbow slotted into the cave of my armpit.

We are a perfect match

our bodies mingle in the colourful aroma
of black & white coffee stains

odours of steel & mirrors
of stones & glass

in a delicate moment
of deep slumber.

Skin

Ronnie McGrath

Skin upon skin
blue like the inky black night
of wild men on wild horses

devilish flames enveloping the skin

hooded men in search of skin

nightmare screams pulling skin
into the irascible charge
of thunderbolt and lightning

polysemic skin wrapped around
my colourless bones

tattooed skin reads like a book

young skin exploited by glamour
aged skin exploited by the lure of youth
female skin years for some lovemaking
unshaven masculine skin blunts razor blades
sexy skin has a price on it

brown skin
gold skin
rich skin
poor skin
skin I'm in skin
skin
    skin
        skin me alive
                if that's what it takes
                    for you to see my humanity

Glenda's Big Decision *(Trinidad 1970)*
Roger Robinson

The one man that she'd had
was all she needed to know.

The approving grunts, the kneading
of breasts. Hot tongue down her throat.

The shoving of her hips, and the clapping
of skin in jerky rhythms, the sting of sweat

in her eyes. The pulled hair, stretched legs,
stale cigarette breaths, the spit, the spit,

the seasoned smell of hard work
deep in his skin. The yellow

in his eyes looking through her,
like hate, like hope, like pride.

The wet slobbering on her neck,
the bites, the suck, the mark,

the lift, the twist, the arched back.
Then the smell; strong, like bleach,

the wetness, slowly snaking its way
down a valley of butt cheeks,

his dead weight pressing down, down
no, no, this wasn't her type of thing;

the slick of it, the sticky thickness of it.
She only chose him because she knew

his mouth was big and years from now,
he would talk of it as if it were yesterday.

What Brenda wanted now was a woman.
She decided that she was going to pay

for one of those Venezuelan prostitutes
all curves, and curls and copper skin

from the Metropol hotel. She had money
from sewing the neighbourhoods clothes,

and that's what she wanted. A woman.
Nodding to herself as she rubbed

the sandalwood perfume into her
wrists and took a long slow sniff.

Hog Plum Tree *(Pleasantville Trinidad 1976)*
Roger Robinson

I was eight, at home with the maid,
Merle, when the yard-man Keith
came inside, already dripping.

 He took off his mud-clumped boots
"A storm's coming small man!"
with a smirk as if it were the circus.

Hurricane Alma came so quickly,
that my parents couldn't get back
to the house, from their town jobs.

Keith whispered something
to Merle who snapped her head
back laughing, then looked at me.

She walked into the bedroom
and Keith stooped down
"Small man, me and Merle

are going in that room to sleep.
So don't bother us. Just watch
TV until we both wake up."

I looked outside the window.
The sky was all bruised cloud
that had turned their backs

and were scudding away.
Mosam's house of black nails
grey wood and rusted–brown iron

sheets, blew away on the breeze
Like some metallic moth.
Then they ran to Shah's house

But his roof peeled clean off
as if lifted by god's can opener;
then they all ran to Mr Beckles.

By now the rain looked
as if I were looking through
it from inside a waterfall

turning houses into ghosts.
I watched my breaths form
in haloed mists of frost.

Loose mangoes were banging
On the metal roof like gunshots,
Then came the squeak and crash

of the fallen hog plum tree and Keith
came from the room holding a green
towel around his waist, slipped on his

boots and tied the towel, and walked
into a hurricane and came back soaking
with two buckets of golden yellow

hog plums. The ones the birds eat
before they dropped. The ones
we could never reach with stones.

Keith and I began to eat hog plums.
and the room smelled like honey,
as the rain tapped at the windows.

Inside the wardrobe
Abdul Jamal

Mummy's left-behind Yardley,
frankincense on Daddy's suits.

A hush. First-time fingers
tube paper to a cigarette.

A match struck in the dark
a blinding orange flame.

A frock's alight, a suit smolders
Mummy is still in the bath.

The pull on a hankie tied with safety pin,
the scratch of smoke in his throat.

Clanging bells, firemen in red.
Neighbours out on Kichwele Avenue.

Jets of water, hissing smoke,
the house is fine.

He stays quiet for days,
learns a new smell of sweat.

First Man Out

(L.G. Hayward 07/02/1907 - 26/01/1970)
Ros Barber

He doesn't have a moustache in the photos,
but he had one once, the furry, tickling kiss
was his: my mental scrapbook of your father
reduced to one goodnight when we were kids.

Here, clean-shaved in Fiji, draped in flowers,
villagers feting those who came by ship,
And here, an on-board bash in dinner jackets,
his eyebrows wild. Nothing on his lip.

That World Cruise, six months in '69,
was all he managed. Retired from a job
it was a blessing he'd survived: briefly free
of the London smogs so thick they'd carry off

the wheezing sort, already prone to cough,
like Grandad with the scrapy, half-shot lung
a wartime exercise gone wrong had left;
a chest too weak to hang insurance on.

Sick, not sick of life – that's why the booze,
to cover up the wheeze inside the laugh.
The Reaper waits at home? You stay out late.
A meal with friends, brandy, a good cigar.

After a lunch date with some friends in Stoke,
your mother snoozing, Grandad at the wheel,
he chose an empty road: the new M6.
An evening doorbell brought you two police.

No-one was prepared. And you, the least.
Dad stayed with us; you travelled up alone,
were handed his wallet, glasses, the car radio
the police removed to stop it being stolen.

You brought it home as if it were his ashes.
As if you'd plug it in and find his voice.

Halloween in Winter
Heather Taylor

At recess, we'd layer into snowpants,
hooded jackets, stringed mittens,
double scarf our faces and slip over
costumes, loose on de-wintered bodies

during classroom hours, that clung
                              to our snowsuits
as we pushed outside to explore snowbanks.
These costumes followed us through
                              photographs,
princesses, wizards, us sweating under catsuits

made to rival Andrew Lloyd Webber
during all-night sewing sessions,
they passed through our family to end
in charity shop bags and other families' photos.

They twinge our memories of night falling
                              early like the snow
as our moms kept vigil by sand salted roads,
blowing breath into hands, stomping feet,
holding Kleenex for runny noses and we,

with glow-in-the-dark bags heavy with candy,
navigated iced sidewalks, barrelled
                              through valleys
made from shovelled paths to ring doorbells
screaming trick or treat, singing, laughing.

Immigrants
Heather Taylor

She was two. Too young to remember
men coming to the door,
calling her father in from fields half ploughed,
the man who fled Odessa and
left behind his German family born to Russia.

All to escape civil war, that midnight long walk
slogging naked through streams,
clothes piled high over heads,
to hide in a train bound for steamers,
the hospitality of unknown Canadian cousins.

The men stood at his door, like the men
                              all those years ago
planted themselves in his parents living room,
the lies growing easier - *er ist tot, der es tat,*
                              das ihnen durch half
(he's dead, who did it, who helped them through)
as they emptied out drawers, his mother holding
                              tight to memory,
the letter they burned saying he was safe.

The men waited at the door,
her father coming in from fields half ploughed
his head playing accordion songs he'd
                              play that weekend
when they raised their neighbours barn.

His English jerked through the screen door,
half the world away from gunpowder and
                              casualty units,
Ich verstehe nicht - he thought he misunderstood
their words: 'We're here for radios, guns.
We can't be too careful. It's a war we're in.
They said you were German.'

from **The breaking of a heart**
– how it is done

Frank Diamand

II The annunciation

She says: *'You'll die alone' Coup* de grace.
An angel blows venom from puffed cheeks.
Four winds rush everywhere to tell
that we don't function anymore.

A swan sails by the ships and the sun
informs that nature with drama
has no thing in common.

The emptiness takes on proportions
                              like *ground-zero*.
Those who die alone salute you!

III

My muse is gone.
She quietly went to sleep
after breaking up with me.
Maybe it is a beauty-sleep
don't know what I'll see at her awakening
still in my bed, but she already works for another.

VI Reasons

Tonight couldn't sleep because of your question
'What was it I did wrong?'
You didn't want my answer, but I did.

Violence you have committed. Because
silence is violence, as lack of trust is
and doubt where language is unambiguous.
Lack of self-confidence,
attributing guilt is, finger pointing is,
not sharing ecstasy is violence.

There are cultures where walking hand in hand
is proof of your fidelity
although you have to wash for hours
to regain your scent.
'Look here I am walking with my beloved!
My lover in a keep-net'.

Not one like that. Survivors are
sharers of backdoors, escape route gliders.

Was that it, I? What did I do, or not do?
Through the leather recognizable forms
condoms in a wallet.
Ostentatious disdain, proven isn't it?
Your pain was impressive and ridiculous.
Nobody is absolutely true, and liberty
is an antidote against adultery.
I didn't screw around, but
choke a walking-bird and it will want to fly.

Forget the above. The heart of the matter…
indifference dismantles love.

Ear

Luke Kennard

The piece missing from his ear makes his ear resemble a corporate logo; I can see that triangular fragment of ear suspended some way out of the notch, as if it were on its way back into the ear to complete it, perhaps to imply that this corporation is the final piece in the puzzle you are trying to solve – and what better symbol of communication than the ear? The ear is used to hear sounds such as dead leaves under heavy boots, a pumpkin being dropped from a high window and whimpering through a thin wall. In some cultures, when someone has been spreading false rumours about you, it is customary to cut off both ears so that everyone else will know that they cannot keep a secret. In other countries this practice has been superseded by the Permanent Hat – a silly looking red cap with a bell, cemented directly onto the scalp. The bell may be cut off, but the hat is impossible to remove. I had my Permanent Hat dyed black and sewn into a new shape, but the results are unconvincing.

Eyes
Luke Kennard

He regards me as if I were struggling to climb a staircase. His eyes are like something you find unexpectedly on the side of a rock, blood-black. I imagine their tentacles unfurling in hunger. 'You can't just kill every insect that comes to you,' he says, finally. 'You can't just sit there at the beginning of Spring, killing every insect that comes to you. There will always be insects. This is not my concern.' A pigeon flies straight into the clean window. I sit perfectly still. 'What I am worried about are the wars going on inside people's heads,' he says. He pats my head, three times, slowly, and looks into my eyes as if he is peering into a malfunctioning hose pipe. 'You needn't worry on that front,' I say. 'I haven't had a single idea in three years.'

Mouth
Luke Kennard

His lip is clean-shaven, his mouth is tidy
like the slot in a piggy-bank. There are no
silent animals; the gazelle and the
antelope and the wildebeest all say,
'Leopard.' They mutter it disconsolately,
under their breath. The General opens a
bronze chest on his desk. Inside it is
divided into several compartments, each
filled with little yellow pills. 'It does not
concern me that you are a liar,' he says.
'Should we, for instance, provide you with
ample opportunity to lie in a harmless,
controlled environment such as your
personal life, I have no doubt you desire
for lying would be sated.' The pigeon
staggers away from the window shaking
out its wings in an accusatory manner.
'A pill cannot make you *care* about people,
but it can make you want to do certain
things to them. This pill,' he picks up one
of the yellow pills, 'makes you want to help
people.'

Failing Light

Lisa Dart

She remembers now the oil stove
more clearly than anything. That and the snow,

and the way the failing light
closed off the sky. But he had been there

and she had thought that day
she would marry him.

She swore she would remember
his raw smell, saltiness,

his white skin, the way he tried
to reassure her,

just as he had the first time
leaving his gold signet ring

by her side when he'd gone off
and slept with someone else.

Instead it's the leaping out of bed
she remembers, the shivering

in the hall when the phone rang,
to learn her niece was born,

the cold sheets on her return,
the bed's stretch of emptiness,

and on the ceiling,
grown large in the snowed-down-dark

the pattern of the oil stove –
its black intricate shadow

that might have been a rose.

Bear

Pierre Ringwald

I thought of my grandson
as the startled mother bear
reared towards me
driven by a maternal instinct
fierce, ruthless,
flesh-and-bone deep.

I thought of my grandson
as I ran towards her roaring bulk
knowing that my survival
lay between her forelegs
out of claws' reach.

I thought of my grandson
beyond the vision of
savage eyes
shifting shoulders of fur

angry teeth.

I thought of my grandson,
imagined the look of wonder on his face
as the balance shifted
in my favour, sending
old man and bear
tumbling down the mountainside.

I thought of my grandson
as the bear retreated, confused
leaving me lying in a crater of snow and ice
drunk on fear and adrenalin

and as I lay there

I wished.
I wished
I could spirit my grandson away
from his world of game consoles
manga
videos
pop stereo
sugar-coated cereal

the neon illusions of Tokyo.

I wanted him
mountainside
his legs pushing through the snow
eager to match my stride
learning the honesty of the elements

slowly

     slowly

          slowly discarding his faith

in headphones
bleeping pocket games
implausibly armed and armored robots

readying himself
to embrace

and tumble
     into
          a world of sudden
               claws
                    and teeth.

By the pool
Alex Brockhurst

I only came to
watch, she said

a finger
tracing along

the fine line
separating

blue dark
eyes, narrowing

the view
that removes her

further out
of bounds

the angular
shift from

restraint
to certainty

I won't go in
just now, she said

Costa Brava
Alex Brockhurst

Eleven forty-five
shutters closed

door ajar
echoes of crockery

and laughter
down the valley

automatic
sprinklers

whisper and
repeat

a sound so close
yet still remote

murmuring
regret

your measured voice
on the terrace below

the gentle mutter
of making up

The Bank
Graham Buchan

Across the river
anglers while away their evening -
redundant men
who have found satisfaction
in not striving.

Fish, I have heard,
have a memory
of only two seconds
so once on the line
they don't regret their life.

I heard that in the nightmare,
post-euphoria '80's,
some sacked yuppies
still lunched regularly
in city diners
unable to give up the gossip.

Above these reeds
a whirlwind of midges:
frenetic energy life process.

In the evening light
a plop -
the float goes under
like Jeremy,
who couldn't hack
his change of circumstance.

Out take
Brendan Cleary

I was squeezing
the wine box
when you called
in a kinda out take
from my cool existence
& I'd stamped on it
squished it about
& thought of Adrian's advice
just cut the corner
with some scissors
& let it slop
so I was relieved
it was nothing serious
you wanted to talk about
not like anybody'd died
not like any horse was running
or you just wanted to hear
the sound of my voice
as if for the first time

Stepping Out
Brendan Cleary

did a runner
with her chums
from the pizza place
just off Middle Street
near William Hills
after 3 carafes of white
& next time I see her
she has bruises
on her upper arm
& doesn't remember
& says she drank
a bottle of whisky
without her flatmates
so I whisper over the bar
gently persuade
her rich brown eyes
'Sarah that'll kill ye
promise me
don't do that again'

Sunday Afternoon
Brendan Cleary

on his 7th pint of Strongbow
he pulls out his mobile
& flashes up a photo
of 'her' in skimpy gear
wearing red leather boots
so I pretend to be envious
& wish the clouds I glimpse
would float down & land
over these aching barstools
& in their softness the sublime
coated all my movements
& at the start of the end
graves never got dug
& lovers never went adrifting

Minaret
Keith Please

At what sky
did an architect
scratch hide,
pause, drawing this:
stone drop
a plumb-bob
and, trembling
mid-air,
sway so far out
the ground itself
took up
and gave it root

or was it always
built upward;
a prayer,
and level of weight
upon weight,
so laying of stone
through the ground
and another upon it,
slowly it grew

or a chance
contrivance of both:
the dumb sling
or stone downward
insisting
on gravity
to what it could bear,
and the thrust
of each cry
up from the ground,
a device
dissolving of sky.

Whale Watch
Keith Please

These are stunning pools,
bubble-net, dance-pod,
veiled ash-green disturbance, air
in water caught, as if all points
from height and depth convene
in softfeed round Stellwagen.

Tundra-black, light of leaf
they've shed disguise and rise
glistening from what, opaque,
they're thought as far above;
by banks below are seen
white stone, a striped white sky.

The whales contain the surface,
up for stills; motionless,
they log a minute, hours
in absorption of a dive,
to re-locate a memory
of long hauls on earth's plate.

Distinct by fluke and fin,
they lie in solitude
ocean, forest
or drift in twos and threes
before lunging into mist
the iris water scatter of a tail.

To Damme and Back
Sarah Maguire

Pacing the towpath of the straight canal,
   once a highway for cloth of gold,
      wool bales, bolts of lace,

now slowed to the traffic of waterfowl,
   squabbling mallards,
      and paired, reflective swans.

Drawn by perspective the water arrows
   clean to its vanishing point,
      ruled by two unbroken rows

of leafless poplars, elegant cages of
                      opalescent air,
   while a soft mist cures the unspoken waters,
      a seam of silver threading these rich,

alluvial soils — polderland at peace on
                      Easter Sunday.
   Damme: once a frantic harbour, next
                   a backwater
      beached by the slow accretions of silt,

now safe with streets of steep-gabbled houses,
   their clean rooms lined with fine china
                  and books,
   overlooking cobblestones polished with mist.

The squat gothic church is shut —
   rooks absolving the huge silenced belfry,
      the gathering bats, gravestones of infants.

We turn round at dusk, walking the known path
   into darkness, retracing the trees, counting
      our steps into five long kilometres.

The freight of ourselves bearing our return —
                              worn bones,
    full lungs, the finite heart, these intricate
                              networks
        of balance and loss carrying us back

as the night turns chill. Side by side our journeys
    divide — youth draws you on, but now
        I am taking the old path home.

White Buildings
Tom Chivers

You sent me a book
in a brown paper bag:
Hart Crane's *White Buildings*,
the cover, a New York skyline in sepia.

A postcard falls out
at pages thirty-
four and -five, your
scrawled marker pen note
leaving a stain in reverse lettering
the same light brown as the filters
on the cigarettes you smoke, although
of course you only do rollups.

'I found this poet on my
travels. Give us a second
opinion.'

Hart Crane's poetry
is clean, concise, no words
out of place. And I guess
you liked that, enough to press
dried leaves between 'Paraphrase'
and 'Possessions'.

In one poem
Hart Crane says:
'There are no stars to-night
But those of memory'.

And I think you would like that too.

I remember you, friend:
the naïve freeness of your laugh
the way you held books and smoked
clothes and hands speckled with dried paint
drinking neat gin and starting to like it
your taste in music and your insistence
on singing along.

You sent me a book
in a brown paper bag:
Hart Crane's *White Buildings*,
the cover, a New York skyline in sepia.

Letter to Barry MacSweeney
Tom Chivers

Dear Barry, today I found you
in a small market town bookshop
between MacNeice and Mahon.

It's the kind of place you'd like;
you'd sit cross-legged in the corner
with Verlaine and a bottle or two,
quite content, dreaming of Sparty Lea.

Later I climbed to the top of a hill:
the landscape opened up,
I could see all down the valley.

It was expected and sudden as fuck.

And you, you knew how to die young
before you did it; it was your
specialist subject.

You'd sit smiling and glowering
in that chair, blacked up all steely SS
with Magnus reeling off names
of rock stars and dead poets,
polite laughter at your little jokes,
and at the end when the credits roll
you'd be gracious in defeat.

But grace was in short supply
when you, hugging the wall, lurched
step by step from your final bow,
whilst genteel applause rang
like the telephone that never picked up
in your jug, bloody ears.

Tyrol *(after Hans Christian Andersen)*
Roddy Lumsden

...where the moon fans shadows of pines
all across the rockface and giant saints
cascade on gable walls: Christopher
toting the infant; Florian dousing
the blazing house; the blood of the Cross
drooling from rooftop to wayside.

Though the paint now speckles and cracks,
and the painters are sprung to dust,
I was there when those muralists swayed,
daring on their ladders, blessing
home after home, each face more pious,
each sword sharper in the Lord's resolve.

On the brow of the crag's brow, the convent
seems a swallow's nest and in the tower
the newest sisters toll the bell; their gazes
fall far, upon a surging coach below
whose post-boy touts his horn and brags
a long note which rises in the dimming light,

rises till it fills a tear flashing in the eye
of the youngest nun who grips the rope
and yanks it down, against herself,
until the speeding horses are distant specks
and the last faint echoes of the horn
are drowned beneath the brazen bell.

Hell
Clare Pollard

'What's it like to be a 21st Century woman?'
Sassy, the girls call out.
Feisty. Opinionated. Independent.
I am doing market-research for anti-perspirant.
I need money for rent.
I am already clenched, closing off, cell by cell –
that lurch of existential nausea.
The group leader can tell
(her brisk smile informs me that I don't belong
with these mojito-messy Carries,
their one-night-stands and spray-tans,
this gang of giggling gal-pals.)
With a thick felt-tip she writes how being
                              single is fab because:
a) you can just be yourself,
and b) you can do what you want without
                    worrying about anyone else,
and c) it is sassy.
Everyone but me decides that, if it were free,
they would have plastic surgery. Mainly boobs.
We make a collage about the kind of woman we
                              imagine uses *Sure,*
chop up *Elle, Glamour, Cosmo.*
The table gleams with girly faves:
Diet Coke, mini-chocs and apples.
'I really love my personality' says the girl
who says she thinks about being skinny
with every cell,
for every single moment of her life.
She is thin. She is as thin as the pics of celebs
that we clumsily snip out of Elle.
The other girls nod.
Pluck at chocolate with their bloodclot nails.
Yes, we love ourselves too.
'What I don't like,' I attempt, 'Is this idea
that just because I'm female I love shopping.
I mean, most women I know have other hobbies
- they aren't that superficial…'

114

A silence, and then:
'I work hard for my money!' the solicitor shrieks.
'If I want to spend it on shoes,
because I like shoes, I *deserve* those shoes.
I'm really offended by what you just said.
That REALLY OFFENDS ME!'
Her shoes are ballet-slippers.
I suppose they are quite nice.
The market-research girl needs answers.
'If *Sure* was a planet,' she asks,
'What would it be like?'

The Lighthouse
James Byrne

We shelved your red Chevrolet,
    above the Atlantic
        and both jumped out –

to pad around in the water
    our two faces lit
        by the lighthouse

From a surveying crag,
    you watched me splash
        in the wobbling foam

and I heard you snigger
    in the background, your voice
        spongy above the sand-swell,

as I lodged my feet
    between a fizz of waves
        that played out their cameo roles.

I called you down
    for a dance low-tide,
        and I still remember how

we tangoed the shoreline
    to imaginary music,
        under that solitary disco-light.

Later the radio packed in
    and all we could do
        was to stare, pre-sleep,

towards the lighthouse,
    with its slow hatchings
        of incandescence.

It was like Hopper:
>the same insistent broom
>>of drooping half-light,

the same vigilant blend
>of beauty and loneliness
>>in its great whirring performance.

Just after dawn
>the light went out.
>>It all happened so suddenly –

was I already asleep? –
>one moment I looked up
>>and there was only sky.

Last I remember
>was you whispering a prayer,
>>something for your mother –

at exactly the moment
>we later discovered
>>cancer finally switched her off.

This was two years ago.
>But you wrote today and said
>>you're driving back to the bay.

You want to know
>if the light has reappeared,
>>to see it again, with clean eyes.

Ros Barber has been poet in residence on the Isle of Sheppey, at Arts Council England offices, and in a barber shop. Her first collection *How Things Are On Thursday* is published by Anvil. Her second collection is due in 2007.

James Bell co-hosts and organises UNCUT poetry in Exeter Recently his *Rumours of Sunlight* was the dedicated feature issue for Poetry Scotland.

Fiona Benson has had poems published in The Feminist Review, Areté, and TLS. She recently won an Eric Gregory award. *Harvest* was previously published as an Oxford Poetry Broadside.

Alex Brockhurst is a visual artist who lives in Brighton.

Andy Brown is the author of six poetry collections, most recently *Fall of the Rebel Angels - Poems 1996-2006* (Salt). The poems here come from *Goose Music* a collaborative book written with John Burnside (Salt 2006).

Graham Buchan's full collection is due from tall-lighthouse in '07. His chapbook *Airport Reading* was published in 2003.

James Byrne's first collection *Passages of Time* was published by Waterways in 2003 & he is the editor of The Wolf magazine. His second collection is due.

Brendan Cleary's has two full collections with Bloodaxe and his latest collection is *weightless* (tall-lighthouse) which was described as a modern blues by Roddy Lumsden.

Tom Chivers is a full-time poetry person running penned in the margins and a ResonanceFM radio show

David Crystal's latest collection is *Just Like Frank*. He has worked as literary editor of *DOG* and his work recently featured at the V&A with artist Ian Pollock. He once read with Carolyn Cassady at the Marquee club.

Lisa Dart was runner up for the prestigious Grolier Poetry Prize in America in 2005 and her pamphlet *The Self in a Photograph* is published by tall-lighthouse.

Frank Diamand is an artist & poet who lives in Amsterdam and has a number of poetry collections to his name.

Isobel Dixon's poetry has been widely published in her native South Africa and her first prize-winning collection was *Weather Eye*.

Carrie Etter teaches at Bath Spa University & for The Poetry School. Recently her poems have appeared in The Liberal, New Writing 14, The Rialto, TLS, Poetry Review and Stand.

Janice Fixter's work has appeared in a variety of magazines and her pamphlet *walking the hawk* was published by tall-lighthouse in 2005. A full collection is due in 2007.

Nell Grey has published three novels as well as poems, short stories, articles and reviews. She's also an artist who finds inspiration when walking her dog on the South Downs.

Lee Harwood resides in Brighton and is described as *one of Britain's best poets and best kept secrets*. His Collected Poems was published by Shearsman in 2003.

Carole Hawkins runs a writing group - The Weyworders and has had work published in small press anthologies, her first anthology *London To Fly For* is published in 2006.

Jack Hayter is a versatile musician, working with the band Hefner as well as with his own album – *Practical Wireless* – he is new to publishing his poetry.

Luke Heeley's poems have appeared in Reactions 4 and Phoenix New Writing and in a number of magazines and online publications. He received an Eric Gregory Award in 2002.

Abdul Jamal is originally from Dar-es-Salaam and his first poetry pamphlet is published by tall-lighthouse.

Rachel Kann is a poet and musician from Los Angeles who is widely anthologised as well as publishing four books of poetry and two cd's.

Luke Kennard's collection of prose poems *The Solex Brothers* is available from Stride Books. His second collection *The Harbour Beyond the Movie* will be published by Salt Books in 2007.

Kim Lasky's poems have appeared in Agenda, Seam and the Frogmore Papers, and she is a past winner of the Live Literature Fresh Talent competition. Her pamphlet *what it means to fall* is published by tall-lighthouse.

Michael Laskey has published three full collections: *Thinking of Happiness* (Peterloo1991) & *The Tightrope Wedding* (Smith/Doorstop1999) short-listed for the TS Eliot & *Permission to Breathe* (Smith/Doorstop 2004). He founded the Aldeburgh Poetry Festival & co-founded & edits Smiths Knoll.

Roddy Lumsden's *Mischief Night - New & Selected Poems* is published by Bloodaxe. A pamphlet, *Super Try Again* (Donut Press) is due in early '07. He teaches at City University and writes for BBC MindGames magazine.

Sarah Maguire is the founder and director of the Poetry Translation Centre at SOAS. Her fourth collection of poems, *The Pomegranates of Kandahar*, will be published by Chatto in June, 2007.

Aoife Mannix's first collection *The Elephant in the Corner* was published by tall-lighthouse in 2005. She is working on her second collection due in '08. She is also part of a two-woman show *accents on words* with fellow poet Heather Taylor. *Broken Love Waltz* is taken from that show.

John McCullough's poetry has appeared in The Rialto, The Guardian, Smiths Knoll and was the subject of a feature in Magma. His new pamphlet, *Cloudfish*, is published by Pighog Press.

Ronnie McGrath's pamphlet *Poems from the Tired Lips of Newspapers* is to be followed by a full collection with tall-lighthouse in 2007. He is also a published novelist.

Jamie McKendrick's latest collection was *Ink Stone* (Faber) shortlisted for the TSEliot. He is the editor of the *Faber Book of 20th Century Italian Poems*

Maureen McManus writes poetry & plays & is Theatre Editor of CEN magazine in East London. Her poetry has appeared in over twenty magazines.

Helen Mort has been a Foyle Young Poet of the year on more than one occasion. Her first volume of poetry is due from tall-lighthouse in 2007.

Keith Please has taught English & American Literature in further and higher education and is published by The Circle Press and in a variety of magazines.

Clare Pollard is a poet and playwright. Her latest collection is *Look, Clare! Look!* (Bloodaxe, 2005)

Maurice Riordan's next collection *The Holy Land* will be published by Faber in February 2007.

Pierre Ringwald is a Canadian in London whose pamphlet *a world of sudden claws* (tall-lighthouse) was PBS choice Summer 2006.

Roger Robinson is one of the most influential black writers in Britain today. His first poetry collection *Suitcase* was published by Waterways in 2004.

Anne Rouse has published three books with Bloodaxe and is currently working on her New and Selected.

Philip Ruthen's poetry and short fiction has appeared in The Poetry Church, Roundyhouse, Nthposition, Cambrensis - Short Story Wales, Psychopoetica. He is book reviews' editor at The Poet's Letter.

Cathy Ryan is new to poetry. Her straightforward style and eroticism is celebrated in her first volume *I dare you* (tall-lighthouse)

Jacob Sam-La Rose's debut pamphlet, *Communion*, was PBS pamphlet choice Autumn 2006. He's been published in Velocity: The Best of Apples & Snakes and other publications as well as being the founder of the Metaroar mailing lists for live literature and spoken word.

Christina Santana is a poet and educator from Chicago, who performs and teaches internationally. She draws inspiration from her Puerto Rican heritage and urban environment.

Maggie Sawkins runs Tongues & Grooves on the South Coast and her work has been extensively published.

Catherine Smith is a Next Generation poet - her first collection *The Butchers Hands* is soon to be followed by *Lip* (Smith Doorstop) early in 2007.

Maggie Sullivan mixes comedy with tragedy in her writing in a uniquely engaging style – her first volume is due from tall-lighthouse in 2007.

Marc Swan lives in Portland Maine. His poems have been published in a wide range of international magazines and volume of his poems is due from tall-lighthouse in 2007.

Heather Taylor is a playwright and poet. Her first collection *Horizon & Back* was published in 2005. She performs a two-woman show *accents on words* with fellow poet Aoife Mannix.

David Trame is an Italian teacher of English, born and living in Venice-Italy. His poetry has appeared extensively in literary magazines. His collection *Re-Emerging* was published by Gatto Publishing in 2006.

Timothy J Wesley has lived in both London & Manchester where he attended the Identity writers workshops, the poem Punch Drunk was written at that time.

Hugo Williams won the TSEliot prize in 1999 with *Billy's Rain*, his Collected Poems was published in 2002 and his latest collection published in 2006 is *Dear Room* (Faber).

Anthony Wilson has just published his third book of poems, *Full Stretch: Poems 1996-2006* (Worple Press) He lives and works in Exeter.

Kathy Wrightson originally from North Yorkshire, now living in London, worked in an arts cinema and for the Arts Council before becoming a social worker

----

tall-lighthouse is an independent poetry business publishing poetry, organising poetry readings and events, facilitating education and learning through training and workshops.

Founded in 2000 we have published more than twenty five books and pamphlets. We organise poetry readings and events in and around London, Brighton and Exeter as well as facilitating writing workshops in conjunction with Arts, Library and Community Services.

www.tall-lighthouse.co.uk